THE MYSTIC NEXT DOOR

THE TRIUMPH OF THE CROSS

Edward Jozsa

"Only God knows the good that can come about by reading one good Catholic book."
–St. John Bosco

Copyright © 2023
by Edward Jozsa

All Scripture texts, prefaces, introductions, footnotes, and cross references used in this work are taken from the New American Bible, revised edition © 2010, 1991, 1986, 1970 Confraternity of Christian Doctrine, Inc., Washington, D.C. All Rights Reserved. No part of this work may be reproduced or transmitted in any form or by any means, electronic or mechanical, including photocopying, recording, or by any information storage and retrieval system, without permission in writing from the copyright owner.

To inquire about speaking engagements, to share your own experience of God, or to obtain additional copies of this book, email:

themysticnextdoor1@gmail.com
or
edjozsa@presenceofGodencounters.com

PresenceofGodEncounters.com

Dedication

I dedicate this book to the Most Holy Trinity and Mary, our mother, who walks with me daily. I thank God for my wife, Amy, and dedicate this work to her for her endless support, calming voice, and the love she gives me. She has never doubted what, for many, would be so hard to believe. And finally, I dedicate this book to my children, Chance, Nate, and Anna. I thank the Lord for them and for their generosity in allowing me to share my time with so many others.

"I will stand at the gates of Heaven, and I will not enter until all of my spiritual children are with me."
– Saint Pio of Pietrelcina.

The Cover

Soon after I returned to flying, I snapped the photo on the front cover of this book from the cockpit of my 767. As I flew into that beautiful sunset, I could see how the horizon represented the world as I now see it. We dwell in that tiny strip of orange, still yet illuminated by the light of Christ.

Above and below that thin line exists two very different worlds. The one below is a tortured pit, where fallen angels and the dammed are chained. The blessed kingdom of the Holy Trinity, full of angels and saints above, extends on forever.

In that faint sliver of light, a battle rages for our souls. The victor of that battle will determine in which world we will reside for all of eternity. The Miles Christi, the soldiers of Christ, are the ones who fight that battle through the power of God and the help of His angels.

Forward

"In my distress I called out: LORD! I cried out to my God. From his temple he heard my voice; my cry to him reached his ears." (Psalm 18:6)

One night, I had a vivid dream. Unlike an ordinary dream, this one was incredibly detailed, and the memory of it has not faded over the years.

I was kneeling on a crimson-red tight-knit runner in the center aisle of a small chapel. The pews were fashioned in a rustic style and finished in a dark mahogany stain. The seats were topped with red pew cushions matching the runner. A rustic wood altar matching the pews stood two steps above the main floor. Hanging on the wall behind it was a matching wood tabernacle.

The true Body of Christ was suspended above the altar in a chalice and host. They were elevated as the priest lifts them at Mass and says, "Behold the Lamb of God, behold him who takes away the sins of the world. Blessed are those called to receive the supper of the Lamb."

The faithful congregation responds in unison, "Lord, I am

Triumph of the Cross

not worthy that you should enter under my roof, but only say the word, and my soul shall be healed."

I was weeping uncontrollably as a stream of tears poured from my eyes and obstructed my view. There lived within me immense remorse and sorrow, much like what I experienced in that place of eternal misery inside the Red Room.

Embedded within that sorrow was a love unlike any other on Earth. It reminded me of the joy and peace I felt in the Presence of the Holy Spirit. I could hear a mournful wailing issuing from my mouth, yet I never paused to breathe. The sorrowful cry continued uninterrupted.

Beside me in the aisle knelt someone else, although I could never fully make out his details through the curtain of tears pouring from my eyes. He was not weeping, and only my cry could be heard. He was very broad and strong, and although he knelt, he looked several feet taller than me. I felt I knew him well and was comforted by his presence. I believe he may have been my guardian angel.

A few feet before us stood a woman in a white dress covered with a deep blue robe. I knew her to be the Blessed Mother, Mary. Her form was obscured of fine detail due to my excessive tears, and her body appeared to shimmer as if heat waves separated us. This effect may have been due to seeing her through my flowing tears, or it may have been due to how her form was presented to me. I could see her in solid form, yet somehow, I could still see the presence of our Lord in the Eucharist through her.

She spoke to me and said, "This is what it is when one's soul is exposed to Our Lord Jesus, the Christ. You cannot help

Forward

but weep a veil of tears when in His presence. And that is what it is, a veil of tears."

I knelt weeping for a time as this overwhelming sorrow and the ultimate love of Jesus permeated into my soul. I understood that these tears were a fusion of my sorrow for my sins and the ecstasy of His love and forgiveness.

I awoke from the dream, feeling the most profound, heartfelt sorrow in the core of my soul. I realized how much the Lord loves us and that we cannot return the immensity of the love He heaps upon us in our mortal form.

One day, we will all enter into an immortal realm, where the Lord will elevate us, and we will become capable of loving Him in a way that is impossible here on Earth.

St. Ignatius of Loyola explained a blessing from the Holy Spirit that he called the Gift of Tears. He said that when one discerns whether something is from God or the enemy, God often gifts us with tears of joy coming from the closeness of the Holy Spirit.

In the dream, the Holy Mother Mary showed me the Gift of Tears. I have often used the Blessed Mother's and Saint Ingnatius' teachings to help me discern God's messages. This dream foreshadowed the encounter I would experience years later while on a pilgrimage to shrines dedicated to the Holy Cross and Our Lady. -Ed Jozsa, February 2019.

"Therefore, you shall love the LORD, your God, with your whole heart, and with your whole being, and with your whole strength." (Deuteronomy 6:5)

Contents

Dedication V
The Cover VII
Forward IX

-CHAPTER ONE-
Ed is Going to Walk 1

-CHAPTER TWO-
Jesus, Mary, and the Tree of Life 9

-CHAPTER THREE-
The Cross in the Woods 25

-CHAPTER FOUR-
A New Heart 35

-CHAPTER FIVE-
Thomas 43

-CHAPTER SIX-
Nikki 49

-CHAPTER SEVEN-
OUR LADY OF CHAMPION...55

-CHAPTER EIGHT-
TREASURES...67

ACKNOWLEDGMENTS...73

–CHAPTER ONE–

ED IS GOING TO WALK

"I am confident of this, that the one who began a good work in you will continue to complete it until the day of Christ Jesus." (Philippians 1:6)

September 14th is the Feast of the Exultation of the Holy Cross, commonly known as the Triumph of the Cross. On this day, the Church celebrates the discovery and recovery of the True Cross of Christ by Emperor Constantine's mother, Saint Helena, in AD 326. On September 12th, 2023, two days before that feast day, my dear friend Terry drove me three and a half hours from my home in Indiana to a gas station outside Toledo, Ohio.

There, I met my new traveling companion, Bud, a man whom I became acquainted with two months earlier. He asked if I would join him on a walking pilgrimage to visit two shrines in Michigan and Wisconsin. The walk would honor the Feast of the Triumph of the Cross and mark the one-year

Triumph of the Cross

anniversary of a project called Operation True Cross (OTC). Terry returned to Indiana as Bud and I, near strangers, departed in a converted construction van. We began a six-hour drive to the tip of Michigan's lower peninsula, our destination, the National Shrine of the Cross in the Woods. Upon our arrival at Indian River, Michigan, the home of the shrine, we scouted the route we planned to walk in the morning and then found a place to eat dinner.

During our meal, we asked the restaurant manager if we could park the van in their lot overnight and explained that it would be our home for the next few days of our pilgrimage. After dinner, we went out to the van and got ready for bed as a thought passed through my mind: This is crazy; what on earth did I get myself into?

The day before the feast day, I woke up on the floor of the construction van at six o'clock in the morning to the sound of Bud's alarm. We prayed the Angelus, a short prayer that meditates on the Angel Gabriel's message to Mary, Mary's fiat, the Incarnation, and the passion and resurrection of Our Lord.

I knew this pilgrimage would indeed have two results: plenty of walking and praying. We prepared for our day and drove to the starting point of our walking journey as I reflected on God's guiding hand and the string of unlikely events that had led me to this place.

Bud Macfarlane Jr. is the founder and president of The Mary Foundation. This not-for-profit organization evangelizes for Christ by distributing books and other materials free of

Ed is going to walk

charge. In February 2023, I mailed Bud a copy of my book, The Mystic Next Door—An Ordinary Man's Extraordinary Encounter with the Holy Spirit. He and a few other men were completing Operation True Cross, a 4,500-mile walk across the country, carrying a relic of the True Cross as a form of reparation for the sins of our nation.

During this journey, these men prayed for the Lord to protect our country from the evil that has beset her. In an email update Bud sent out to his benefactors early on in the journey, he talked of his team's many trials and tribulations. He called the men walking with him Cyrenes because they carried the True Cross as Simon did, helping Our Lord carry His cross.

When I read Bud's message on that cold winter morning, I thought he and his companions might find solace in reading my first book since I had spent so much time writing about how important it is for each of us to carry our cross for Christ.

I shipped a copy of the book to the Mary Foundation. Eventually, I forgot about sending the book, but I never forgot about the Cyrenes carrying the cross for our nation. I often thought about how much I'd like to help carry that cross, but I knew for my broken and disabled body, it would be impossible. Realistically, the state of my physical status mattered not since it was doubtful I would ever have the opportunity to meet Bud, let alone carry that cross.

In July 2023, I received an email from Bud's son Xavier, the general manager of the Mary Foundation, informing me that he had read my book. He invited me to come to Ohio and record a podcast with him. A week later, I drove to Cleveland to record with Xavier and another Foundation employee, Anthony.

After our recording session, I met other Mary Foundation workers, including, to my surprise, Bud Macfarlane Jr., who was cordial and very generous. He gave me several sets of his novel series written earlier in his life and other evangelization products that the Foundation ships worldwide.

Five minutes was all the time Bud and I had to get to know each other, and he told me that once the podcast was published, he would give it a listen. Shortly after, I was on my way to give a talk to a young adult group Xavier and Anthony were involved with. I headed back home the following day, glad I had met the folks at the Mary Foundation, but I never expected to see any of them again.

A few weeks after my visit, Bud called me, asking if Amy and I would join him for dinner in Cleveland. "I listened to your recorded podcast, and I want to ask you a few questions," he explained.

Amy and I drove back to Ohio three days later to meet Bud at a restaurant. After our meal and enjoyable conversation, Bud offered me an opportunity to meet him the following week for a two-day conference at Our Lady of the Holy Spirit Center in Norwood, Ohio, where he was scheduled as the keynote speaker.

I agreed to meet him there, and as we were saying our goodbyes that night, Bud paused and asked, "Do you think you could walk with me for one last short leg of Operation True Cross?"

Ed is Going to Walk

Without any hesitation, before I could even process his question, Amy blurted out, "YES!"

My mind tried to process all the factors as I noticed Amy and Bud were staring at me, waiting for my reply. Finally, I offered a very reserved "Yes."

Once Amy and I were alone in the car, I asked, "How on earth will I be able to do this physically?"

"Eddie, I am certain God is calling you to this walk. He will give you the strength and help to complete it."

I met Bud at the Holy Spirit Center in Ohio a few days later. After he spoke that evening, he introduced me to a group of people involved in the Our Lady of Light healing ministry. They asked if they could pray over me and ask God to heal me. I agreed and sat down as the group readied themselves for prayer. One of the women on the healing team knelt, pulled up the legs of my trousers, and pulled down my socks.

I've only experienced a healing ministry one other time, and it was nothing like this. Honestly, her behavior took me by surprise as she was frantic and kept repeating, "I need to bless his feet; God is telling me, 'Ed is going to walk.'" She anointed my feet and ankles with oil and then stood to join the others.

As the group prayed over me, a great peace came into my soul, but afterward, I was still slightly disturbed by the lady's actions. Bud had assured me in advance that he would keep our walk secret, but now I wondered if he had told the healing team about our pilgrimage.

I approached Bud, and before I could say a word, he said,

Triumph of the Cross

"That was kind of strange that she knew you were going to walk."

"Bud, did you tell anyone about our walk?"

He assured me that no one besides Amy and his team back in Cleveland knew of our plan.

A few moments went by, and the woman approached to talk. "I'd like to apologize." She continued, "I'm so sorry; I have never experienced anything like that before. God was calling for me to anoint your feet, and He kept telling me that you would walk. All I knew was that it was important to God that I anoint your feet."

Amazed, I thanked her and replied, "It could only be by the voice of God that you knew I was going to walk. I am indeed going on a very special walk. Thank you for obeying God's call."

When I returned home from the conference, Amy decided to help me start "training." Since my auto accident, I have not been able to walk for more than ten minutes at most before "the wheels come off the train," and my body breaks down.

I think training is probably too intense of a word since the distances would be considered extremely minor for the average person. She and I started slowly, only walking for a few minutes on many training days. One day before I left for the trip, we were able to walk about a mile. However, each short or shorter walk ended the same way. I limped back into the house and collapsed into my chair for the rest of the day.

As I trained to prepare my weakened body for the pilgrimage, it was evident that if I walked any distance with

Ed is going to walk

Bud, I would need much help from God.

"Now the one who has prepared us for this very thing is God, who has given us the Spirit as a first installment. So we are always courageous, although we know that while we are at home in the body we are away from the Lord, for we walk by faith, not by sight." (2 Corinthians 5:5-7)

-CHAPTER TWO-

JESUS, MARY, AND THE TREE OF LIFE

"Jesus spoke to them again, saying, "I am the light of the world. Whoever follows me will not walk in darkness, but will have the light of life." (John 8:12)

The weeks passed, and as I continued to prepare physically, the Lord prepared me spiritually. I wouldn't make those spiritual connections until the first day of my pilgrimage. As I mentioned in my first book, sometimes God gives me these silent lectures called locutions. They are often posed mentally as questions I don't know the answer to.

During my morning prayers on one of those training days, I was asked, "Washed clean in the blood of the Lamb?"

My answer, as usual, was, "I don't understand; explain it to me."

While there are often words of explanation, it is as if I am learning by seeing, and the knowledge is infused into my mind. I rarely hear words spoken; rather, they are placed in my mind. I'm aware that while I may be the subject to whom the knowledge is directed, the knowledge applies evenly to everyone.

Through this infusion of knowledge, I was shown that one day, I will stand before Christ and see myself in His Truth through His eyes. There will be no hiding my faults or covering up my sins; everything will be exposed. I will see my true self for the first time.

Then, I was shown the red room again and the horror I spoke of in my first book. This new lesson was being presented to help me understand that first vision. In this new vision, I stood before the Lord, my God. I loved Him as I had never loved before with all my heart, mind, and soul, as sudden horror overwhelmed me. I knew that the only way for me to enter the Kingdom was through Christ's mercy, and I understood that His mercy came at a great price for our Lord.

Sin builds a blemishing scale on our soul; perhaps this blemish is more like a callus as it separates us from God's touch, causing pain that cannot be felt in our physical bodies. As I stood before Christ, I knew that for me to enter into the Kingdom, He must remove that scale—that sin—and take it onto Himself. I became intimately aware that my sin, which I once believed held no real pain, was going to cause extreme spiritual pain and anguish for my Lord. Yet He willingly desired to take it on Himself because Christ desperately wanted me to enter into and live in eternity with Him.

Jesus, Mary, and the Tree of Life

"For our sake he made him to be sin who did not know sin so that we might become the righteousness of God in him." (2 Corinthians 5:21)

Then I was shown the red room from my previous vision, and once again, I felt that white-hot burning in my soul—the regret, the misery, and the soul-crushing sorrow. Only then did I understand that my sorrow, misery, and regret resulted from my knowledge of the staggering spiritual pain Christ must suffer for me. It was too late to change anything, and it was too late to avoid the sin of my life. If only during my earthly life I had understood what my sin did to our Lord, I could have kept Him from suffering so deeply. However, I had chosen sin over virtue, and my Lord and I both would suffer because of my past choices.

My love for Jesus was beyond anything I ever imagined; however, for me to live with Him, Christ had to suffer. I loved Jesus as my God, Savior, Brother, and Friend to a depth I had never fathomed before, and I was aware that my sin would cause Him pain to a degree I also had never fathomed before. For me to finally realize that I was the reason that my Lord had to suffer such pain was additional torture for me.

In that previous vision, it wasn't until I let the Lord take on all my sins that I was lifted up through the red liquid that moved within the ceiling above me. In that vision, my eyes were fixed upon that blood-like liquid throughout my existence there, and I could never look away from it. After I passed through, I found myself in that lush, peaceful meadow, looking up into the bluest of skies.

Triumph of the Cross

I was back in my chair with my daily prayers in my lap, as a distant memory formed in my mind of another locution where my gaze was fixed on the Lord. The memory was too far off to recall, but it would ultimately return to me during the pilgrimage.

The following day, once again during my morning prayers, the Lord reminded me of yet another message given to me earlier that summer. I saw no correlation between the frequent messages presented then, but it would soon be revealed. Still, in reflection after returning from the trip, I realized the Holy Spirit had been working diligently to prepare me spiritually for what lay ahead.

Then I remembered the question that was asked of me the month before: "Why were Adam and Eve cast out of the garden?"

I answered, "Because they ate of the tree of the knowledge of good and evil."

I was told that was not the entire answer. They were also cast out at that moment in time because God did not want them to touch the Tree of Life or eat its fruit–yet.

I was skeptical about what I heard. My answer came from a Scripture verse that I was sure I knew. I felt I was being led astray. But afterward, I searched the Scripture and found that what I thought I knew was incomplete.

"Then the Lord God said: See! The man has become like one of us, knowing good and evil! Now, what if he also reaches out his hand to take fruit from the tree of life, and eats of it and

Jesus, Mary, and the Tree of Life

lives forever? The Lord God therefore banished him from the garden of Eden, to till the ground from which he had been taken." (Genesis 3:22-23)

Then I was told: when Christ came, God made Man, there became a new heaven, a new earth, a new Adam, a new Eve, a new Fruit of the tree, and therefore, also came a new Tree of Life, which is the Cross. While God once cast us out because of his concern we would touch the Tree of Life before we were ready, He now invites us to touch the new Tree of Life daily. It isn't only that God wants us to touch it, but we must eat of its Fruit, Christ in the Eucharist. We must embrace the new Tree of Life daily, deny ourselves, and pick up our cross to return to Him in the Kingdom.

"Then Jesus said to his disciples, 'Whoever wishes to come after me must deny himself, take up his cross, and follow me. For whoever wishes to save his life will lose it, but whoever loses his life for my sake will find it.'"
(Matthew 16:24-25)

"Jesus said to them, 'Amen, amen, I say to you, unless you eat the flesh of the Son of Man and drink his blood, you do not have life within you. Whoever eats my flesh and drinks my blood has eternal life, and I will raise him on the last day. For my flesh is true food, and my blood is true drink. Whoever eats my flesh and drinks my blood remains in me and I in him.'"
(John 6:53-56)

As I got up from the floor of the OTC van, these lessons from my past were a million miles away from my thoughts

Triumph of the Cross

My focus and concern were to not disappoint Bud and the rest of the OTC team if I physically failed to complete the last leg.

We drove to a secluded railroad bed that had been converted into a trail—the starting point we had scouted out the previous day. This rail-trail would cover the first six miles of the eighteen-mile walk that day.

The model for the last two years was for two Cyrenes to leapfrog, with one man walking and the other driving ahead to a safe pickup spot. The man walking wore the relic of the True Cross, and whenever roles were switched at the transfer spots, he would pass the True Cross off and pray over the other man.

Bud let me start first to take advantage of the smooth trail and quell my excitement about carrying the cross. The path I walked on was beautiful, and on both sides grew a lush Michigan Northwoods forest. Oak, maple, and birch trees lined the railroad bed on both sides.

As I departed on that scenic trail, I offered a prayer of thanksgiving. I thanked God for letting me walk. The thought, Dead Man Walking, came to my mind because that's what I was in more ways than one. I should have died in that multi-car crash, but the Lord saved me. Where my physical self should have died, it didn't; my spiritual self was reborn, and the man I once was, indeed, was gone. As I took those first few steps, I realized I was embarking on the impossible. Before Bud dropped me off, I told him that I planned to walk two miles, twice as far as I believed I could.

Prayer wells up in us from God, and a prayer came into my

Jesus, Mary, and the Tree of Life

mind. I understood in the fullness of time from the Father's perspective, I walked carrying the Cross at the exact moment Christ carried it 2,000 years ago. From the Heavenly Father's view outside of time, Jesus and I were carrying the True Cross simultaneously.

I asked Jesus if He would allow me to carry the full weight of His Cross so that He could walk beside me without His burden. Almost immediately, I felt the presence of Christ walking with me, shoulder to shoulder. I expected to feel a staggering burden, but I felt lighter than usual, stronger, and my pace quickened.

After a few more minutes of walking down the path, the locution of the Tree of Life came back into my mind. Only now, I saw the events of Adam and Eve's expulsion playing out like a movie in my mind. I still felt Jesus walking beside me, although He remained silent and unseen. I knew He was allowing me to see the events in the garden as they unfolded. I was able to watch the serpent tempting Eve with the fruit all the way through God's expelling the couple and placing the angels to guard the Tree of Life.

The last scene played out, and I became aware of my surroundings again, still walking on the old railroad bed. I felt Jesus urge me to stop walking, and without a conscious effort, I found myself stopped on the path, facing the woods on the side of the trail. Two feet in front of me was an apple tree full of luscious ripe fruit.

I was amazed; this tree was in the most unlikely of places. There were no other fruit trees—only the mature trees of the deep woods. I laughed at how good the apples looked

Triumph of the Cross

and said aloud to Jesus, "There is no way I'm taking one of those." I stared at the tree and felt the strongest urge, almost a longing, to pick and eat one of the apples. I resisted the urge and stepped away; Jesus continued walking quietly beside me.

As I proceeded along the path, I considered the unlikely timing of finding a fruit tree as the story of Adam and Eve ended. With that thought, I noticed another presence walking beside me. Jesus was still on my left, but walking on my right was His mother, Mary.

I walked quietly with the two of them, pondering how often Mary and Jesus must have walked together, and I wondered what they might have talked about on those journeys. I was enjoying their company and the immense peace engulfing me when a touch of sadness crept in. I realized that my time walking with Jesus and Mary would all end as soon as I reached the rendezvous point with Bud.

To track my walk, I used an app on my phone that would sound an alert and give me my progress when I completed each mile. The mile alert sounded, stating my average speed was 3.3 miles per hour. I had used this app during my training, and I could never break 2.6 miles per hour. My current pace was the equivalent of an all-out sprint, not to mention the distance I had already trekked. I had not walked that far in over six years!

I was in total disbelief that, physically, I was still feeling fine! A walk like this back home would have me crawling into my chair, ruined for the rest of the day and probably the next. Earlier, I asked Jesus to give me His Cross, but it felt

Jesus, Mary, and the Tree of Life

like He was carrying me. I had no other explanation for the record-breaking pace and distance.

We continued down the path together when I noticed Mary had fallen behind while Jesus was still walking beside me. She was lagging behind our pace several feet back. "Lord, is Your mother okay? Why has she slowed down?" Jesus gave me no answer.

As we walked on for a few minutes more, Mary was now twenty yards behind us, still following but falling farther behind. With more urgency this time, I asked, "Why is Mary so far behind? Should we wait for her? Is she okay?"

Before the last words passed through my mouth, my body failed. All those injuries, which had kept me from walking at home, flared all at once, stopping me on the trail and preventing me from taking another step. A slight panic overcame me. I was in the middle of nowhere and unsure how I would get to the designated pickup point. While those thoughts flooded me, I felt Mary slowly catch up to where Jesus and I were standing.

Mary then spoke four words into my mind. "You're walking too fast!"

Mary, who always cares for and intervenes with her Son on behalf of all her children, tried to slow me down, but I didn't listen. I laughed as I thought about how her words reminded me of her words at the wedding at Cana. I've always loved the mother-Son exchange in that story. Mary knew the Lord best. From before His conception and through His life, ministry, Death, Resurrection, and Ascension, Mary had been there with Him.

Triumph of the Cross

At the wedding, Jesus asked Mary why He should be concerned that the groom and bride had run out of wine. Mary had already known since that day long ago when she and Joseph had found Jesus in the temple that Jesus would do whatever she asked of Him. I can almost see her gentle smile and loving wink toward her Son, never breaking her gaze upon Jesus as she tells the servers to listen to Him.

"When his parents saw him, they were astonished, and his mother said to him, 'Son, why have you done this to us? Your father and I have been looking for you with great anxiety.' And he said to them, 'Why were you looking for me? Did you not know that I must be in my Father's house?' But they did not understand what he said to them. He went down with them and came to Nazareth, and was obedient to them; and his mother kept all these things in her heart." (Luke 2:48-51)

"On the third day, there was a wedding in Cana in Galilee, and the mother of Jesus was there. Jesus and his disciples were also invited to the wedding. When the wine ran short, the mother of Jesus said to him, 'They have no wine.' And Jesus said to her, 'Woman, how does your concern affect me? My hour has not yet come.' His mother said to the servers, 'Do whatever he tells you.'"
(John 2:1-5)

I stood on the trail for a few more seconds, and the pain that had overwhelmed me faded away. I started my walk again, but slower than when I began. Jesus and Mary were still there, one by each shoulder, walking with me as I continued

Jesus, Mary, and the Tree of Life

on the journey.

Another twenty minutes down the trail, I could see a bend in the path ahead where a country road and the path crossed. The van was parked on the side of the road, and as I approached it, Jesus and Mary were no longer beside me.

I arrived at the van and looked at my app. I had walked nearly two and a quarter miles and still felt surprisingly well. The memory of my walk with Jesus and Mary has not faded, and I will always cherish my time traveling with them.

I handed the cross to Bud and was urged to give him a message. I told him that he was to walk without earbuds and to pray no rote prayer. I told him that in God's timeless sight, he would carry the Cross at the exact moment that Jesus carried it. I told him that he needed to walk in silence and listen. I prayed over him, and then he departed on his first leg.

I drove to the next transfer spot, a little over six miles away, and I prayed quietly while I waited for Bud to arrive. A couple of hours later, Bud made it to the transfer site, and by then, I felt refreshed and rested, with only minor aches. I was sure God was granting me an incredible grace. So many of the gifts God has given me can only be described as impossible, but I prefer to call them miraculous.

When Bud walked into the transfer spot, he asked, "Do you feel you can walk another leg?"

After a serious evaluation, I felt I could walk another two miles, even though this would be a more difficult leg. We were off the railroad bed, and I would be walking on the

Triumph of the Cross

berm of a winding and hilly two-lane highway.

So much for peaceful meditation because now I was focused on the semi-trucks as they screamed past me. I used Mary's lesson from my first segment and walked slower than before. As the walk wore on, I could feel my body approaching its limit, but thankfully, as I turned a corner, the van was waiting on a side road right in the nick of time. I had walked just over two miles for the second time that day!

We had one more walk to complete and would be at the Shrine of the Cross in the Woods. It was Bud's turn, with just over six miles to go. The plan was for me to drive to the parking lot and wait. Once Bud arrived, we would explore the shrine together.

I added, "Bud, I want to walk the last half mile with you. When I get to the parking lot, I will rest, and if I feel I can, I'll walk out to meet you. Would you call me when you are a mile out? God willing, maybe we can meet and finish the last leg together."

Bud agreed to call, and we parted ways, both headed for the Cross in the Woods.

When I got to the shrine, I parked the van and walked over to a park bench on the edge of the property. I didn't want to venture further since we planned to explore the place together. I rested for a little while and offered God another prayer of thanksgiving. I could hardly believe I had walked over four and a half miles that morning. Although my feet were sore, the rest of my body felt in good shape. I thanked God again for the incredible gift He had given me. After finishing my prayer, I sat quietly when the silence was

Jesus, Mary, and the Tree of Life

shattered as a bold thought crowded my mind.

I knew I had to tell Bud about the Tree of Life locution, and I had to tell him now! Sometimes, the Lord places a thought in my mind, but I try to wriggle out of it. I foolishly tell myself all the reasons why I shouldn't listen. I discount the thought as just me being crazy, or worse yet, I don't want to complete a difficult task the Lord has asked of me. God was not having any of it this time. I glanced at the clock and knew Bud was still too far away. But it didn't matter; I had to get to him and tell him the story.

I started walking away from the shrine in the direction where I had left Bud, knowing I would eventually meet him. The question bombarding my mind was, Can I walk that much farther today? The steps passed by faster and faster, and I pushed myself even harder as the minutes ticked away.

What God asked made no sense to me, but I knew I had to tell Bud this story. About twenty minutes and nearly a mile later, Bud called to tell me he was a mile out, as I saw him approaching from the other direction.

I crossed the road, anxious to tell Bud the story, but before I could get a word out of my mouth, he said, "Thanks for suggesting I walk in silence. Nothing big happened, but I feel that we should skip Mass here at the Shrine today. We can travel during daylight to the Shrine of Our Lady of Champion this afternoon. We can attend Mass there in the morning. I think we should get there today."

Honestly, it didn't matter where we stayed that night, and while I wanted to go to Mass, it didn't matter on what day or in what town we attended. I brushed it aside, agreeing quickly to whatever Bud wanted because I had to tell him the story of the Tree of Life. I told him word for word about the message, and his reaction was the same as mine the first time I heard it.

Bud said, "That isn't why they were expelled from the garden..."

I cut him off, "I said the same thing when it was explained to me, but I looked it up, and Scripture does indeed confirm it."

Bud asked if I had a Bible on my phone, so I opened my Bible app, found the verses about the Fall, and handed him my phone. He read, backed up, and reread the verses. Then, he returned the phone to me, pulled out his own, and found and reread the Scripture. A few moments later, he put his phone away and said, "How is it that I'm a sixty-year-old man and have studied Scripture for most of my adult life and missed that passage the whole time? Bud then read the verses out loud,

"Then the Lord God said: See! The man has become like one of us, knowing good and evil! Now, what if he also reaches out his hand to take fruit from the tree of life, and eats of it and lives forever? The Lord God therefore banished him from the garden of Eden, to till the ground from which he had been taken." (Genesis 3:22-23)

We started walking again, and Bud said he would need to think about this message and pray for a while to discern what it meant. I knew that Bud was a very spiritual man, well-versed in theology, and I trusted his knowledge of Scripture.

Jesus, Mary, and the Tree of Life

I wondered if the urge I had felt was just my desire for him to help me discern if the message given to me was valid. In any case, I was happy that the sense of urgency had been satisfied with my telling of the message, and I was at peace, feeling that my job was done. We were both completely unaware of what the Lord had planned for us back at the shrine.

We finished the walk into the shrine and rested at the van as I added up the total of our walks that day. Bud racked up over thirteen miles that morning, while I came in at just under half that with six. I don't think the walk was challenging for Bud. He had just finished walking 4,500 miles over the last year, so that day was probably a piece of cake for him, but it had been more than six years and another life away since I had walked six miles.

I skirted away from the van to hide the tears that began flowing when I saw my total. They were tears of thanksgiving for the miracle God had granted me. Walking six miles in less than six hours is medically and physically impossible for me.

"For nothing will be impossible for God."
(Luke 1:37)

-CHAPTER THREE-

The Cross in the Woods

"Deep calls to deep in the roar of your torrents, and all your waves and breakers sweep over me." (Psalm 42:8)

The Shrine of the Cross in the Woods is stunning. The forest surrounds it, and the grounds have paths that weave through the trees, leading to a giant steel cross fifty-five feet tall. Upon the cross is a twenty-eight-foot-tall bronze corpus of Jesus. After Bud and I rested, we left the van to explore the shrine. We brought Daily Prayers to Save America booklets printed by The Mary Foundation.

We stopped to pray when we got to the foot of the cross. Once we finished, Bud said he wanted to enter the chapel and bring his relic of the True Cross to the true presence of Christ in the Eucharist. We searched for a while inside the chapel but could not find the tabernacle, a vessel used to house the Eucharist outside of Mass. The tabernacle provides a location where the Eucharist can be kept for the faithful's adoration and later use, and it prevents the profanation of the Eucharist. Just as we were about to give up, Bud called out, "Here it is! It's in its own Adoration Chapel."

Bud was ahead of me and entered the chapel before me. The chapel was fitted with commercial steel doors with push bars, as you would expect to find in any large commercial building. Inside, the room was small, with barely enough space for Bud and me to be in there together. Bud is a big guy, tall and thick. He was walking in front of me, and I could not see the tabernacle.

Bud unexpectedly turned to face me with his mouth ajar. As he turned, he stepped aside and pointed to the tabernacle. I was so surprised by his quick turn and the look on his face that it took me a moment or two before I looked at where he was pointing. Forged on the doors of the tabernacle was the Tree of Life!

I have been a Catholic my entire life, and since every Catholic church has a tabernacle, I've probably seen hundreds in my lifetime, and likewise, the same is true for Bud. He asked, "Have you ever seen a tabernacle inscribed with the Tree of Life?"

I could barely speak, as my mind was spinning, and I answered quietly, "No." I had been passionately motivated to tell Bud about the Tree of Life less than an hour before. I knew telling him about the message was urgent then, but I didn't understand why. The Lord wanted me to tell Bud before we saw the tabernacle. I was both amazed and incredibly humbled to witness the mighty hand of God at work. The thought overwhelms me as I am reminded of just how small I am every time I see the Lord work through me.

Although I had only known Bud briefly, we had enjoyed

The Cross in the Woods

several worship opportunities together. We attended Mass together, as well as Adoration of the blessed Eucharist, where I witnessed Bud's deep reverence for God. When Bud is in the presence of Christ in the Eucharist, he prostrates himself; that is, he lies face down in homage to the Lord. This day was no different.

I knelt on the kneeler, which was placed just out of reach of the tabernacle, as Bud prostrated himself on the floor next to me. A moment after I knelt, Bud reached up and placed his relic of the True Cross by me on the armrest of the kneeler. Thinking he was giving it to me, I picked it up, bowed my head, and placed the Cross against my forehead.

A thought came into my mind, and I asked Jesus a question in prayer. "My Lord, how long has it been since You were this close to Your Cross?"

And then I was gone! I knew my body was still kneeling in front of the tabernacle, but I could also see myself as if I were viewing the scene from above and behind, treading water in what looked like an ocean of mercury—vast and smooth with no shoreline. I knew my soul was now separated from my body; above and behind me, one body was kneeling by the tabernacle, while at the same moment, my body was also in the ocean in front of and below my soul. A perfect descending line could be drawn connecting one body to the other, with my soul placed squarely in the center of the two.

One second, I was focused on myself treading water, and the next, I was no longer observing from above but was living the experience from within the water. I felt a small wave of spiritual pain crash over me, submerging me. Describing this

Triumph of the Cross

spiritual pain is challenging to put into words, but it felt as though my soul was being torn apart. I wanted to scream at the top of my lungs but could not. The pain submerged me, and I could hear my body on the kneeler, gasping for air.

My body on earth struggled to breathe as my body in the ocean went under. I realized this was not just a vision; this spiritual experience also affected my physical body. I understood that in the hospital after the wreck, the Lord had let me feel the physical pain of His Passion, but as awful as that was, it paled in comparison to this new pain. Christ suffered both physical and spiritual pain for our salvation, but at that moment, I realized His spiritual pain was infinitely the greater of the two.

Much like when I was in the presence of the Holy Spirit, God infused His knowledge into me again. I knew the small wave that submerged me was the wave of pain Jesus felt because of my sin. I could see the correlation between the white-hot burning in my soul when I suffered in that Red Room so long ago. I understood for us to be washed in the Blood of Christ, He feels the horrendous spiritual pain I was experiencing.

I finally realized that while I was in that Red Room, in that purgative state, I suffered because it pained me to know my sins were causing such agony for the Lord. The pain my sin caused Him was the reason I carried such regret because it was too late for me to do anything to lessen the suffering I caused Him.

These thoughts came to me in an instant, but before I could take my next breath, another wave of spiritual pain crashed

The Cross in the Woods

against me, submerging me. This wave was more significant than the first and pushed me farther under the surface, causing my body on the kneeler to gasp for air again. The waves came larger and faster, washing over me and driving me under with each subsequent crash.

With each wave, I could hear myself gasping for breath on earth while my body in the ocean shuddered from the pain. I felt myself reaching out with only my right arm for something barely out of reach. I was frantically trying to grasp the item to help me pull myself up out of the waves to save myself. But whatever I was reaching for remained unseen and out of reach. As the waves grew, so did the pain they carried, and each one became more unbearable than the last. The pain was agonizing, but I felt something buried deep inside the pain that rode along within the suffering.

I could feel that same love that I once felt coming from the Holy Spirit, which touched me like rays of sunshine then. Now, this love wasn't just touching the outside of my soul; it was penetrating deep into the interior and structure of my spiritual being.

My soul felt like the pain was tearing it apart, yet the love was so pure and good that it made all the pain worthwhile. I felt the love that Christ poured out for us in His Passion, and to call it beautiful does not begin to do it justice. I know of no earthly words to describe it. The waves kept coming, each bigger and stronger than the last, and as they increased, so did the pain they carried, but in proportion, so did the love.

I knew the first wave resulted from my sin, and the following waves were the combined effect of all the world's

Triumph of the Cross

sins throughout the ages. This was the suffering Jesus accepted and the love He poured out for us. The physical pain that I felt in the hospital so long ago did not even register on the scale when compared to the spiritual pain I felt. Strangely, as horrible as it was, I didn't want it to end because I knew the love flowing within it was rebuilding my soul, and I didn't want to lose that feeling.

I suddenly became aware that my body kneeling at the tabernacle was dying. I had not taken a breath in a very long time, and I was drowning, suffocating under an ocean of sin and the pain caused by that sin. How strange it would be for people to find me dead from asphyxiation, I wondered. Would they find water in my lungs if an autopsy were completed?

Then I heard a voice say, "No more." I'm not sure if it was my voice or another, and it reminded me of the Prayer of Union that the Holy Spirit had shared with me. At that time, the only word I could say was "More." And now all I heard was, "No more."

> *"Out of the depths I call to you, Lord; Lord, hear my cry!*
> *May your ears be attentive to my cry for mercy. If you, Lord,*
> *keep account of sins, Lord, who can stand? But with you is*
> *forgiveness and so you are revered."*
> *(Psalm 130:1-4).*

Once I heard those words, everything stopped, and I was back again, kneeling in front of the tabernacle, still holding the cross to my forehead. I was about to fall unconscious as I took a deep breath, the first in a long while, and I noticed the

The Cross in the Woods

telltale signs that I was recovering from a near blackout. My vision returned as the black tunnel faded with each additional breath I drew. I could feel the excruciating pain slowly drain away from my soul as if it were water, but something had changed within my soul. I could still sense the otherworldly love residing not just in it but throughout it. I felt as though my soul had been completely rebuilt.

Tears were streaming down my face, and although my sight had returned, the tears obstructed my vision. I tried to stand up, and while my body rose, my arms were fixed to the kneeler. The cross weighed a thousand pounds, and I could not lift it.

I knelt back down and used the kneeler for support. I pulled the cross close to my chest, and by pushing off with my legs and elbows, I managed to stand. The weight was unbelievable, and my legs shook with every step; I was crashing into the walls, staggering out of control from one side of the room to the other under the tremendous weight of the cross. Earlier in the morning, I asked the Lord to let me carry the full weight of His cross, and at that moment, I experienced that weight.

When I finally reached the steel doors at the chapel entrance, I could not open them because I held the weight of the cross tight to my body with both arms. I lowered my shoulder to exert pressure on the door's push bar. I must have looked like a running back breaking through the line as I crashed through the doors that separated the quiet, little chapel from the crowded lobby. The other visitors milling around turned with a jolt to look at me. I was completely

TRIUMPH OF THE CROSS

off-balance and plowing through a line of folding chairs, knocking them askew.

I realized Bud must have left at some point because he wasn't next to me when I returned from wherever I went. I was desperate to get outside and find him. I saw the exit doors, and I started to stagger toward them. It seemed as if hundreds of eyes were watching my every move with grave concern. Then I felt a strong hand firmly grab my arm and lift me as he asked, "Are you all right, buddy?"

I blurted out, "Take the cross!"

Bud replied, "No, you're good; you can keep it."

I growled, "It's too heavy; I can't carry it."

Bud easily took the cross from me as if it weighed nothing and led me outside to a park bench as he asked. "What happened?"

Before I could answer, he said, "When I prostrated myself, I realized I was lying on the crucifix. I thought I shouldn't let it touch the ground, so I placed it on the kneeler next to you. I didn't expect you to pick it up. Before I got up, I could hear you gasping for air, and it sounded like you were dying, so I stood up. Then I saw something that I can't explain. Your right arm was thrust straight out, holding the crucifix a few inches from the tabernacle. Your grip on it was so strong that the cross looked like it was shaking. Your knuckles were white from squeezing it so hard."

I was utterly exhausted and barely had the strength to talk, so all I could get out was, "I went somewhere. Jesus let me feel the spiritual pain of His crucifixion, at least as much as a

The Cross in the Woods

person could endure."

At that very moment, I realized something had changed in me. I want to say it was a physical change, but I'm not sure physical is the right word for what I experienced since the soul is not a physical element. In any case, my soul was now different.

Ever since the experience of losing God's touch on my soul in that place of eternal misery, sorrow, and regret, amazingly, I have been able to feel His hand holding my soul. After this encounter, I could feel Christ's love carried within those waves of pain and poured into my soul, still dwelling within me. Not only could I feel the love, but I felt as if the walls of my soul were rebuilt, and His love was infused in their being.

A flash came into my mind, and a quick vision of my heart appeared. I could see that the wall muscles were now changed as if they were made of another substance—no longer the same. I knew that my physical heart had not changed, and what was shown to me was offered as an example of what the Lord had done to my soul.

Once the vision of my heart ended, I quickly recovered, though my arms, back, and legs were still shaking and sore from carrying the incredible weight of the cross. Bud helped me up, and we walked back to the van, ready to continue our trip through the Upper Peninsula of Michigan to the Shrine of Our Lady of Champion in Wisconsin.

Triumph of the Cross

"I will sprinkle clean water over you to make you clean; from all your impurities and from all your idols I will cleanse you. I will give you a new heart, and a new spirit I will put within you. I will remove the heart of stone from your flesh and give you a heart of flesh. I will put my spirit within you so that you walk in my statutes, observe my ordinances, and keep them."
(Ezekiel 36:25-27)

-CHAPTER FOUR-

A New Heart

"The LORD will fight for you; you have only to keep still."
(Exodus 14:14)

It was a beautiful autumn day for traveling, and I was thankful we had decided to change our plans to depart in the early afternoon. I had never driven through that part of the country and was looking forward to seeing the north-country forest and Lake Michigan. We weren't long into the drive when I realized something truly had changed in me.

Bud started giving me a recap of the sequence of events. He did this more to get everything straight in his mind rather than for my benefit. He said, "You told me to walk in silence, and I felt drawn to change our plans and leave for the next stop today rather than tomorrow. You left the shrine early with the need to tell me about your locution of the Tree of Life, and then we got to the shrine and found an incredibly unique tabernacle with the Tree of Life carved into it. I placed the relic of the True Cross next to you, and before I knew it, you sounded as if you were dying. I looked at you, and you

Triumph of the Cross

were holding the cross out in the most fascinating way."

A moment passed as I took in all that he had recited and seen. Before I could answer, Bud said, "You had another experience; you went somewhere."

While Bud was reviewing the events, I couldn't help but notice my soul. In the past, as a result of the experiences surrounding my auto accident, on occasion, at God's choosing, He would grant me the grace to feel other souls. I could never read their souls, as it was said that great saints such as Padre Pio could. Mostly, I could sense when a soul was in pain, or on rare occasions, I could feel a soul filled with Christ's loving peace.

Now, I could feel Bud's soul, and my soul swelled in reaction to his. Christ's love that remained in the structure of my soul knew Bud intimately, and somehow, because of His love, I also knew Bud as a result.

We drove along as Bud continued to rehash the events, and I noticed that I could feel the people passing us in their cars and the pedestrians walking on the side of the road. I would feel a flash as I watched a passing vehicle, and I knew and loved the driver for a brief moment. Then again, flash! I saw a woman walking on the sidewalk, and I knew her and loved her for a second. Over and over, as fast as we drove by others on the road, I knew them and loved them in my soul.

Not wanting to make contact with anyone else, I looked at the floor of the van, feeling strange—as if I were an intruder breaking into all these private lives. Still, I knew and loved them like they were my family. I looked up, and for the sake of their privacy, I turned my focus onto Bud. We had about

A New Heart

five hours of driving ahead of us when something urged me to tell Bud about another message I had received years earlier about the spiritual battle.

I was happy to share the experience since it would occupy my mind, and I could let the strange yet peaceful, newfound feelings in my soul rest for a while. I told Bud I wanted to tell him about the spiritual battle as it had been shown to me. This was my vague memory of gazing upon the Lord, which came to me during my training for the pilgrimage but now became bright and clear in my mind.

Like so often when the Lord shares His messages with me, this one began as a simple one-word question; "Fear?"

The message behind the question was then revealed to me.

Fear is a powerful tool the Enemy uses against us, so much so that God has told us, "Be not afraid..." more than any other command in Scripture. The Enemy and his demons take advantage of our propensity for fear and use any situation they can for the ruin of our souls. In our fears and vices, they find a steed to make their warhorse. In 2020, I was shown a vision of the spiritual battle as it engulfed the world at that time.

I saw myself on the battlefield of life; my generals and commanders had all fled except for a scant few, and there I stood, a mere private—a foot soldier—with no weapon in my hand. I was wearing little clothing, barely enough for modesty, totally exposed. The enemy, mounted on a mighty battle stallion, a warhorse, sat high above me, only a few feet away. That fear now turned stallion was the pandemic, and the enemy used his steed to strike fear into the hearts of many

Triumph of the Cross

to intimidate and cause capitulation.

With an ugly snarl, he barked, "I've closed your churches; what will you do?"

Although I was physically alone on this battlefield, my guardian angel guided me to look over my right shoulder, and behind me, I saw Jesus, sitting calmly and comfortably relaxed. He sat in the most indefensible position as if the devil and this great battle horse were nothing to Him. Our Lord had not a shred of concern.

In a soft and loving voice, Jesus spoke to me and said, "Yes, Eddie, what will you do?" The fact that He used the name Eddie struck me deeply.

I had grown up addressed as Eddie, and not until I was an adult did I start introducing myself as Ed. My family, wife, and friends from a half-century ago still refer to me as Eddie, so I'm not sure why it surprised me that my God, who remembers me from before my birth, would call me by my earliest name.

As I turned back to face my adversary, I realized that he could not see or hear Jesus; he believed I was alone and defenseless. I never addressed him during this encounter.

I realized my counterattack was to attend Mass in person, so I told Jesus I would find a way to attend Mass in the real world. The enemy heard my answer. After my exchange with Christ, the enemy's strike was defeated. I could see that he was as perplexed as I was at my defensive blow. My answer to Jesus defeated his attack.

Somehow, the adversary knew he had lost that round,

A New Heart

and his next attack came from atop his stallion. He snarled again, "I have removed your sacraments, your Eucharist, your confessions, your baptisms, weddings, and funerals. What will you do?"

Again, I looked over my shoulder, and Christ asked in his loving and peaceful voice, "Yes, Eddie, what will you do?"

I turned back to face the Enemy again and thought to myself, answering only Jesus, I will receive the sacraments, but more importantly, I will demand they remain available. I was becoming bolder in my thought, and again, the enemy felt my defensive strike.

This battle raged in the same way, volley after volley. He retaliated each time, full of hate and contempt, snarling a question. Then Jesus, full of love and faith, again questioned me.

Our Lord had such faith IN ME. Christ's belief in and love for me emboldened me. I realized that Christ was the one who fought my battle, and all the while, He sat relaxed, completely unseen by the enemy. Christ pounded him without effort or ever lifting a finger.

I was reminded of my time with the Holy Spirit, where I had witnessed His staggering, infinite power. I remembered the contempt I had then for the enemy because he let his pride control him. I was a mere mortal, yet I knew that no one or thing could ever defeat the power of God.

The following two attacks came quickly with snarls, "I removed your holy water." Then, "I removed your song of praise."

Triumph of the Cross

I responded the same way as before. His defeat continued each time as I looked to my God and answered only Jesus' questions in my mind. I will work to return them both.

Not until later did I realize I had never answered the enemy. His assaults caused me to look to Jesus, listen, and respond only to Him. I chuckled at what this battle must have looked like from atop that horse. I never said a word to the enemy, but with every attacking question, I looked over my shoulder and then turned back toward him, silent as if I were ignoring him.

His final attack was far different from the first. I felt like he was now negotiating for a small victory. Once large and intimidating, his stallion was small, weak, and sickly; the armor hanging from the pony's back looked worn and damaged. He was slumped in the saddle and looked small and defeated. His armor was dirty, dented, and in shambles. He began his last feeble request with a pitiful swipe, saying, "At least wear the mask as a sign of your fear of me." His request felt like a resignation of defeat as he disappeared, and the vision ended.

"For, although we are in the flesh, we do not battle according to the flesh, for the weapons of our battle are not of flesh but are enormously powerful, capable of destroying fortresses. We destroy arguments and every pretension raising itself against the knowledge of God, and take every thought captive in obedience to Christ."
(2 Corinthians 10:3-5)

A New Heart

As I contemplated this experience, I thought of Matthew 28:20, when Jesus told us He would be with us always. Christ and my angel were with me on that smoking battlefield. The fact that I am not any different from any of God's other children has always been made known to me. He is with us all, and this lesson on the battlefield was meant for all of us. It demonstrates that when engaged in the spiritual battle, we must focus only on Christ and answer only Him.

The Enemy will use anything he can—fear, addiction, pride, confusion, or whatever we are attached to in an unhealthy way—as his warhorse to confront us on the battlefield. Little does the Enemy know that our Father, our Brother, our Friend, our Love, our God, and our Savior rests easily behind each of us in our private battles. Jesus says, "This is my army; the gates of the enemy will not prevail against their assault."

"Do not fear: I am with you; do not be anxious: I am your God. I will strengthen you, I will help you, I will uphold you with my victorious right hand."
(Isaiah 41:10)

I wasn't sure why I needed to share that locution with Bud, but as we drove along, we shared stories of how God had worked in our lives. Bud's stories proved what I could feel in his soul: he was a good man, truly working to bring as many souls as he could to the saving grace of our Lord. Although we didn't know it yet, we were about to meet a few souls in desperate need of God's grace.

"And behold, I am with you always, until the end of the age."
(Matthew 28:20)

–CHAPTER FIVE–

THOMAS

"With firm purpose you maintain peace; in peace, because of our trust in you." (Isaiah 26:3)

We drove over the Mackinac Bridge, leaving the Lower Peninsula and crossing into the Upper Peninsula (U.P.) when Bud said, "They have a food here called pasties or something like that; look it up." I searched on my phone and quickly found the answer.

"They are called pasties, and they're meat pies specific to the U.P."

Forty minutes later, I was admiring the striking scenery of Lake Michigan off the left side of the van and the deep Northwoods to the right. While I was staring into the forest, Bud made an unexpected sharp left turn with wheels screeching. We came to a sliding stop in a small gravel lot as dust drifted over the van and the small building at the edge of the lot.

In front of us was a small cottage used as a rest stop, with

Triumph of the Cross

a few other cottages a short distance away. I gathered my things, which had scattered with the abrupt halt, and looked at Bud with a questioning glance, a little perturbed at the unannounced and unplanned stop.

Answering my look, he replied innocently, "I noticed a sign posted that says they have pasties. Since we were talking about them, I stopped."

As we walked into the store, we were greeted by an older gentleman. When Bud asked his name, he barked "Thomas" in response.

Bud followed with, "Are you a believer?"

"A believer in what?" Thomas growled even louder.

"You know, are you a Christian?"

Thomas went off. "I'm a businessman, and you don't stay in business long talking about religion." He became enraged, as if a boulder had been released from a high peak and was picking up speed and power. Bud tried to defuse the unprovoked tirade, but Thomas wasn't listening.

Everything slowed down for me. I knew Thomas; I could feel his soul, and I knew what he wanted to talk about. I felt as if I had all the time in the world to learn about him and prepare a list of questions for him.

I interrupted his enraged harangue and asked, "Are these your cabins?" I pointed to the cabins scattered about the property.

Still enraged, with his eyes fixed on Bud, his voice sounded like a deep growl as he replied, "Yes."

"Do you have a beachfront?" I asked.

Thomas

"Yes," he said, his anger starting to drain away as he reluctantly looked away from Bud and turned toward me for the first time.

"Is it rocky? I noticed the beach right down the road was quite rocky." I said.

"Nope, not mine. It is rocky where you saw it on the other side of the property," Thomas answered. His chest puffed up as he smiled and spoke pleasantly for the first time. "We have a sugar sand beach just a short walk from the cabins."

"Thomas, my friend and I are Catholics on a pilgrimage coming from the National Shrine of the Cross in the Woods in the lower part of Michigan, and we are on our way to the National Shrine of Our Lady of Champion in Wisconsin."

Though he responded in a gruff voice again, he was still smiling. "That's not the Shrine of the Cross; the real one is up here in the U.P."

I could see a physical change come over him as he gently said, "I used to be Catholic, and every summer, my grandparents would take me to the Shrine of the Cross not far from here." He pulled a map off the wall to show Bud and me. "We used to go camping every summer and visit the shrine. You two need to go to that shrine." Thomas' mind drifted, and I could tell he was back at that shrine in his youth as his smile grew even more prominent.

A few moments later, I knew it was time to bring him back, so I asked him if he liked to read. He answered that he did, and I offered to give him a copy of my book, just as Bud told me to run out and get one. I came back into the store and

Triumph of the Cross

handed a book to Thomas.

At times, when I've given the book to a person, they stare at it in deep silence as if they can feel it—almost like they are reading it without opening the cover. Thomas followed suit. He promised to read it as we paid for our pasties and returned to the van.

Bud started to drive again in silence. I was deep in thought, trying to figure out what had happened. Whatever it was, I knew calming Thomas was the result of Christ's love woven into my soul. I also understood that I didn't calm that man; rather, Jesus' love for Thomas gave him peace.

Bud startled me from my reverie when he asked, "How did you know what to say to him?"

"I knew what he wanted to talk about." I left it at that.

We continued our drive through the countryside, sharing deeper conversations about God. I was then prompted to share something with Bud that I have told very few people. Since my experiences after that devastating crash, the Lord has granted me some special graces, and one such grace is the gift of suffering for others.

"Now I rejoice in my sufferings for your sake, and in my flesh I am filling up what is lacking in the afflictions of Christ on behalf of his body, which is the church." (Colossians 1:24)

At the Lord's choosing, He allows me to carry another's pain to give that person relief. I cannot control this grace, which does not manifest through my desire. Like all good things, it is initiated by God. Jesus asks us to pick up our cross and carry it, but He never asks us to carry more than we can.

Thomas

Occasionally, we grow overwhelmed while carrying our cross—possibly from fatigue or after suffering a defeat in the spiritual battle. Often, when I encounter someone struggling with their cross, I hear a small voice give approval and say, "Go ahead." I know then that God is asking me to offer to carry their burden for a while.

> *"O Lord, my God, I cried out to you for help and you healed me." (Psalm 30:3)*

And if those tired souls allow me to take their burden for a while, they feel God's peace and enjoy relief for a time. The burden is never as heavy as I expect it to be because I know Christ carries that pain, and I am only an instrument of His mercy. There is always a limit set on how long I am allowed to bear someone's troubles, and once that period of time ends, a moment of absolute humility and joy washes over me. I am no one, yet the Lord lets me witness and feel His mercy. As I often explain, no words can begin to describe the glory of the Lord.

> *"But rejoice to the extent that you share in the sufferings of Christ, so that when his glory is revealed you may also rejoice exultantly." (1 Peter 4:13)*

—CHAPTER SIX—

NIKKI

"And whoever does not provide for relatives and especially family members has denied the faith and is worse than an unbeliever." (1 Timothy 5:8)

We drove on for several more hours, finally arriving at the shrine of Our Lady of Champion in the early evening. We scoped out the area and looked for a suitable walking route for our last day and one final leg of Operation True Cross. Bud and I consulted our phones to search for a dinner restaurant. A penance we observed during our pilgrimage was eating only one meal a day at dinnertime, with only small snacks for breakfast and lunch.

We chose a place, and Bud drove while I put the destination in my GPS. Our Lady's Shrine is in the middle of beautiful Wisconsin farm country where houses are few and far between, and restaurants are even more scarce. My head was lowered as I read aloud the menu of our chosen eatery.

I nearly yelled as the van shot off the road again to the left, brakes squealing and gravel flying once more. We came to

Triumph of the Cross

rest in the lot of a small roadside bar. As I looked at Bud in disbelief, he said, "Let's eat at this place; it's closer."

We walked into the bar, which was like a movie scene. I could imagine the sound of a record needle being dragged to a stop. The three patrons, the bartender, and the lone waitress at the little bar seemingly weren't expecting anyone else since everyone was already there and sitting in their usual seats. No one told them we were coming, and I wasn't sure how welcome we were until the waitress greeted us with an excited smile. "Hi, I'm Nikki. Grab any table you want. I'll be back with some menus."

Bud and I looked around and picked one of only two booths in the place while the gentlemen at the bar accepted our presence and returned to their conversations. A few moments later, Nikki returned with the menus and glasses of water. Then Bud asked her the same question he had asked Thomas earlier. "Nikki, are you a Christian? We're Catholics, and we're on a pilgrimage."

Nikki said, "Are you here for Our Lady's Shrine?"

Bud answered, "Yes," while I was thinking, She must be familiar with the shrine since it was just a few miles down the road. This bar probably gets many visitors since it's the closest eatery around.

But Nikki's following words proved me wrong: "I grew up Catholic." She put her foot on an empty chair, pulled up her pant leg, and showed us a remembrance tattoo of an older woman surrounded by rosary beads. She continued, "This is my grandmother, and when I was a little girl, I used to say a Rosary with her every day."

Nikki

I felt a sadness come over her, and Bud also picked up on it. "Nikki, what is troubling you?" He paused, then added, "My friend and I are going to walk as a form of penance tomorrow, and Ed will carry your pain for you as he walks. I know it sounds strange, but it's something he does."

No one had ever offered this grace on my behalf before, probably because not many knew about it. Will God let me carry her troubles since He wasn't the One Who offered it? I wondered. Then, a thought struck me. Today, Bud had seemingly and randomly chosen places for us to stop...but now I wondered if he was being led. When he felt the urge, he had changed plans—even while driving 50 miles per hour. Something had been guiding him to bring us to people in need.

Throughout our trip, Bud kept telling me he wasn't a mystic, but I was beginning to doubt that. Saint Ignatius of Loyola contended that we are all mystics and can see and experience God much more than we usually expect.

Nikki looked from Bud to me and then back to Bud again as she started crying. She told us that her grandfather had Alzheimer's and that he lived hours away. She was the only one who could care for him, and she was leaving her job and her home to live with him until he passed away. I felt so much sorrow, fear, and hopelessness in her. Just as it was with Thomas earlier, I knew and loved her soul because Jesus knew and loved her.

Bud and I talked with Nikki for a while, and our conversation ended with me asking her if she liked to read. She told me, "Yes." At that exact moment, Bud suggested,

Triumph of the Cross

"Give her a book."

I returned from the van with a few books to share with Nikki, her grandfather, and the other patrons in the bar. She mentioned that the others there that night wouldn't read it, but I encouraged her to offer them the books anyway.

She silently stared at the cover for a minute or two when she took the book. This was the second time I had seen a person react to the book that way today. It looked as if she were reading it without opening the cover. It occurred to me that had Bud not unexpectedly swerved into this bar's parking lot, we would have never met this young woman in such need of our prayers.

Bud and I paid our bill and drove back to the shrine's parking lot, our home for the night. Bud commented, "Pretty cool that we met those people today who needed help. Does this always happen to you?"

"No, not to this extent."

At times, I know the Holy Spirit is working, and I'm encouraged to say something, but these meetings were on another level. While encountering these people in such spiritual need, I was somehow given a glimpse into their souls so that I could say exactly what God wanted them to hear.

I fell asleep with tears in my eyes. I was in absolute awe of the Lord and humbled beyond measure that the Lord would choose a sinner like me to do His work. I was just some regular guy, and I could think of billions of other people more deserving than me.

Nikki

"For we are his handiwork, created in Christ Jesus for the good works that God has prepared in advance, that we should live in them." (Ephesians 2:10)

-CHAPTER SEVEN-

OUR LADY OF CHAMPION

"Come to me, all you who labor and are burdened, and I will give you rest." (Matthew 11:28)

I woke up on the floor of the construction van at six o'clock in the morning to the sound of Bud's alarm. I thought of yesterday's events and asked myself, Could it have only been one day? Did everything that happened since we started out together occur in only one day? Bud interrupted my thoughts as he started reciting the Angelus prayer.

The sun was coming up as we got ready for the day, and it looked to be another nice one. The Shrine of Our Lady of Champion sits on well-kept grounds with walking paths, trees, and ample park benches. From the van, I could see one of the secluded benches bathed in the early morning sun, so I gave Bud some space and moved to that bench to say my morning prayers.

For me, there is something special about praying in the sunshine. When I was in the presence of the Holy Spirit, I could feel the love and mercy of the Holy Trinity touch

Triumph of the Cross

me like rays of the sun. While being in the sunshine isn't nearly the same, it remains a peaceful reminder of my time with God, so when I can, I pray outside in the sunlight. This morning was perfect; it was a crisp 45°, cool enough for the sun to warm me but not cause me to overheat. Before I knew it, hours had passed. They offered the sacrament of Penance at ten o'clock before Mass, and I wanted to attend both.

"And when he had said this, he breathed on them and said to them, 'Receive the Holy Spirit. Whose sins you forgive are forgiven them, and whose sins you retain are retained.'" (John 20:22-23)

"Is anyone among you sick? He should summon the presbyters of the church, and they should pray over him and anoint him with oil in the name of the Lord, and the prayer of faith will save the sick person, and the Lord will raise him up. If he has committed any sins, he will be forgiven." (James 5:14-15)

After my confession, I returned to another bench near the chapel to pray. Suddenly, a thought came to me that I had to find Bud. I could have begun my search in any one of the several buildings on site, but I was drawn to look inside the administration building. I walked into the main doors of the office building, and I saw Bud standing at the other end of the lobby.

He looked at me as if waiting for me and said, "Oh, good, I was looking for you. I want to introduce you to someone."

I thought, Well, that was pretty quick and easy. We walked

Our Lady of Champion

into a small side room, where I saw a woman sitting with Bud's relic of the True Cross on her lap. She was looking down as her tears fell onto the Cross. Bud said, "Ed, I'd like to introduce you to Teresa; I've let her hold the Cross for a while."

I'm not a very touchy guy, and I rarely touch others besides my wife and kids, but as I approached Teresa, I knew I needed to place my hand on her shoulder as I said, "Teresa, I want to offer you the peace of Christ." I couldn't believe what I heard coming out of my mouth, and I thought, Can a regular person even offer the peace of Christ? Doesn't that have to come from the Lord? Is it mine to give?"

My thoughts were instantly disrupted because as soon as I had spoken, Teresa broke out into a loud sobbing wail. I immediately regretted what I said and thought, I just received the answer to my questions since my words obviously upset her.

It was getting close to Mass time, but once again, Bud suggested I give Teresa a few of my books, so I performed the routine trip to the van to bring in books for someone Bud encountered. I handed Teresa the books, and she looked at the book like the other two people we met—as if she were reading it through the cover. Bud reminded me that we needed to walk to the chapel for Mass. I said, "Go ahead. I need to talk to Teresa for a minute."

Bud received the cross back and left for Mass.

When I first met Teresa, I felt she needed Christ's peace, but now, I could sense pain and hopelessness in her soul. Her burden was so heavy—even to the point of crushing

Triumph of the Cross

her, so I asked her if she would let me carry her pain. Teresa immediately told me no, but I pushed her on it.

"Teresa, God sometimes allows me to help others carry their burden. He has built and trained me for such moments. Would you give your pain to me just during Mass? When Mass ends, I will return it to you. I promise that carrying it will not hurt me like it does you. Maybe you can find an hour of peace."

With some hesitation, Teresa agreed as fresh tears came, but they weren't tears of pain. I could feel a change; her tears reminded me of my own whenever God was especially close to me.

"Bear one another's burdens, and so you will fulfill the law of Christ." (Galatians 6:2)

I quickly found my way to the chapel as Mass began and sat beside Bud. Usually, when I offer to carry someone's pain, I feel something, but I didn't feel anything this time. I was sure that God was asking me to help, but I must have discerned poorly, as I felt nothing out of the ordinary.

When it came time for the priest to give his homily, my heart nearly stopped. The priest started talking about the New Adam, the New Eve, the New Tree of Life, and the New Fruit hanging on the Tree.

The priest's sermon was nearly word-for-word, the exact message I had been pushed to tell Bud only twenty-four hours before. Meanwhile, almost every sentence the priest spoke caused Bud to look at me in disbelief or to elbow me in amazement.

Our Lady of Champion

When the priest finished, I tried to gain my composure and focus on the Mass. As the Mass continued, I noticed a slight discomfort on my head, and it reminded me of the feeling one gets after taking off a hat worn all day—just a sensation around my skull as if I were wearing a hat that was too small.

The discomfort grew, becoming steadily worse. I now got the image that my head was in a circular vice, squeezing tighter and tighter by the minute. I could no longer focus on the Mass, only on the growing discomfort, and my thoughts returned to Teresa. I feared that she, or perhaps one of her loved ones, might have brain cancer; all I knew was that her pain was coming from some head illness or trauma. The Mass ended, and so did the vice-like pain, affirming for me that what I felt was indeed Teresa's pain.

After Mass, the priest announced we had an extraordinary opportunity to worship a relic of the True Cross. He explained that the act of worship is the correct term. Catholics venerate, defined as "regarding with great respect, objects that have religious importance, such as the Blessed Mother Mary or the relics of saints," but he said we worship the True Cross. We worship the True Cross because our Lord's blood seeped into it, and being of a natural fiber, the wood of the cross absorbed Christ's blood into itself. Because the blood of Christ permeates the fiber of the cross, it is His blood held within the wood that we worship.

I looked at Bud, and this time, I elbowed him, whispering, "That's cool that they are allowing you to present your cross for the congregation." I assumed that was why Bud was in the office building earlier and must have set this up before

Triumph of the Cross

meeting Teresa.

Bud answered, "I didn't know they were going to expose my cross. The priest must have heard that we have it with us today." We were both surprised and excited that everyone at Mass would have the opportunity to pay homage to the Lord through Bud's relic of the Cross.

The priest continued his talk. He said that a benefactor of the Shrine had recently loaned a relic of the True Cross to be adored in the chapel as he began to uncover a reliquary. This receptacle held a separate relic of the True Cross. Once again, during our short time of worship at Our Lady's Shrine, Bud and I turned to look at each other in utter shock.

We had seemingly spent the entirety of the last 24 hours in complete amazement. At that moment, a thought crossed my mind that I would write about this short pilgrimage one day. The thought also occurred to me that God was providing His amazing grace so often and in such grand displays that no one would ever believe me if I wrote about it. I couldn't help but think of those love stories played around Christmastime where everything lines up and works out in the end because of a Christmas miracle.

Indeed, we were undoubtedly witnessing God's powerful guiding hand. I then asked God, "Gracious Lord, could You please tone it down, just a little, to make it more believable? If I'm going to tell Your story, no one will believe it, and they will think I've watched too many love stories."

My prayer saddened me. No one could witness what Bud and I had seen and have any doubt that they were witnessing the hand of God working in the lives of the people we met along our way. But I knew how skeptical the world has become, and I knew that God was giving me the opportunity to allow people to understand that He works this much, if not more, in each of our lives every moment of every day. Why shouldn't we expect our life to be a love story written by a Creator Who loves us more than we could ever understand?

"God added his testimony by signs, wonders, various acts of power, and distribution of the gifts of the Holy Spirit according to his will." (Hebrews 2:4)

Bud and I waited until the very end of Adoration of the Holy Cross before we moved forward to worship at the foot of the Cross. I carried Bud's relic around my neck, and as I knelt in front of the other relic, I touched Bud's to it.

It was quiet in the chapel as I held those two pieces of the True Cross together. Like the day before, a thought came into my mind, and I wondered, How long has it been since these two pieces were together? I felt as if two long-lost brothers had been united through the centuries together again, and a feeling of peace came over me.

I realized that this was the Feast of the Triumph of the Cross. In my hands, I held the tool of salvation into which our Lord Jesus poured His Blood. Farther in front of me was the tabernacle, where the real presence of Christ lived. That tabernacle was placed within a beautiful shrine erected to honor His mother, Mary, the living tabernacle who also held within her the living presence of Jesus.

When we finished our worship, Bud left the chapel while I remained behind to sit silently and ponder the thoughts swirling in my mind. My concentration was interrupted, and for the second time that day, I knew I had to find Bud. I got up, looked at the three exits on the different sides of the church, and walked out the main door farthest from me. I emerged from the chapel and saw Bud, who was a short distance away, talking to Teresa.

A thought passed quickly through my mind, That was easy...again. And I smiled to myself.

As I approached them, I could hear Teresa and Bud laughing, and I was overjoyed to see her happiness. Before Mass, she was full of sorrow and pain, but now she felt lighter and joyful. I told her how happy I was that she was smiling and laughing. I had forgotten that I had offered to take her pain until she thanked me. Suddenly, my memory was jogged, and I was reminded about the vice I felt around my head during the Mass.

Fearing that she or a loved one was suffering from a brain illness, I asked, "Teresa, do you have an illness, or does a loved one suffer from a brain illness who needs prayers?"

With slight hesitation, Teresa said, "No..." but with a questioning tone.

"Teresa, it was strange, but during Mass, I felt as if my head were in a vice, and it just kept squeezing harder and harder; I thought maybe someone had a brain issue in your family."

With that statement, the joy and happiness drained from Teresa's face, and tears started flowing as she let out a sorrowful cry. Whatever peace she had felt was now gone, and I was sick to my stomach to be the cause of her misery. It seemed everything I said to this poor woman triggered her tears. I was beside myself.

Teresa explained, "My husband is obsessed with how he will care for our family in the event of calamity. His fixation is to the point that it is ruining his life and having an ill effect on our entire family." She paused for a long time as I remained dumbfounded in silence. Before I could say anything to comfort her, she continued, "He says that the obsession feels as if his head is in a vice, and there is nothing he can do to free it!"

I realized that while I carried her pain in Mass, her pain stemmed from the love she held for her husband and the pain his obsession caused him. My answer to her came without effort, and I listened as if someone else was speaking. "Tell your husband no man can solve his problem and prepare his family—not him, not me, or any other man on earth. He needs to come here to this chapel and attend the Mass at this place. Christ is the only one who can take your husband's burden. Christ is the only one who can properly care for his family. I felt your husband's pain, and he must know that only Christ, present in the Eucharist, will free him from that obsession. When the priest elevated the consecrated Body and Blood of Christ, the pain in my head departed."

"When you pass through waters, I will be with you; through rivers, you shall not be swept away. When you walk through fire, you shall not be burned, nor will flames consume you. For I, the Lord, am your God, the Holy One of Israel, your savior."
(Isaiah 43:2-3)

Triumph of the Cross

"The Lord will rescue me from every evil threat and will bring me safe to his heavenly kingdom. To him be glory forever and ever. Amen." (2 Timothy 4:18)

Teresa stopped crying when she heard those words. I felt hope coming from her soul. I hugged Teresa, and we parted ways. Then I turned to find Bud. He had moved a short distance away after I first approached him and Teresa, and as I walked up to him, he said, "I'm glad I walked away."

I knew he was referring to her loud cries, so I explained, "It probably didn't look like it, but Teresa and I had a good conversation."

"Ed, we haven't had a chance to talk since before Mass. When you walked into the office building, I was looking for you so I could introduce you to Teresa. The next thing I knew, you were there." He stopped momentarily before continuing as if something just dawned on him, and he asked, "How did you know Teresa needed Christ's peace?" Thankfully, before I could answer, because I had no answer, he continued, "When I met her, I told her I had a relic of the True Cross and asked if she wanted to hold it for a while. She sat down, placed it in her lap, and started weeping, and her tears fell onto the Cross. She said, 'I just want to feel the peace of Christ.'"

He continued, "Then you came in, and that was the first thing you said."

I didn't have an answer, but like the other times since I felt the spiritual pain Jesus suffered in His Passion and the love that reconfigured my soul, I knew Teresa when I met her.

Our Lady of Champion

We discussed the priest's homily and the nearly word-for-word retelling of the story I shared with Bud the day before. We talked about how unlikely it was to see a tabernacle with the rare depiction of the Tree of Life engraved into it. We discussed the decision that had brought us here today to Thomas, Nikki, and Teresa, who needed to feel Christ in their lives.

I've thought about how, at times of the Lord's choosing, I can feel the soul of others. God loves us and knows us better than we will ever know or love ourselves. Perhaps when I experienced the spiritual pain that He suffered and the love carried within that pain, it somehow stayed with me. Maybe it is a remaining gift that allows me to witness how much Christ knows and loves us all and that He wants His peace to live within each of us. By sharing what He showed me, I am blessed to be allowed to share His love and peace with others and to remind them of what Jesus told us in John 14:27:

"Peace I leave with you; my peace I give to you. Not as the world gives do I give it to you. Do not let your hearts be troubled or afraid."

Bud and I found a quiet park bench on the shrine grounds to repeat the prayers for the country. Before we started, Bud said, "You know, you are really like a child." Even though I knew what he meant, he quickly clarified. "Not in a bad way. You know, like in Matthew 18 verse 3, 'Amen, I say to you, unless you turn and become like children, you will not enter the kingdom of heaven.'

He continued, "You're like that—simple and childlike."

I didn't know how to answer, but it was as if Bud blew my

secret wide open. My whole life, I've felt like a child. When I was a young boy, I knew I was a child to be seen and not heard, but even as I grew older, I couldn't shake the feeling that I was still just a kid.

I'd often find myself talking with a group of men and women, hoping they didn't discover I was just some kid and didn't belong at the grownups' table. I was an airline captain in command of a 220-million-dollar aircraft carrying millions of dollars' worth of cargo all over the world, yet I still felt like a child. I was surprised to finally meet someone who could see me for who I was. In any case, I took Bud's observation as a compliment and wondered if perhaps God used that childlike quality to help me with His mission.

We finished the prayers and departed for the last walking leg of Operation True Cross. This time, we would walk together in a circular route covering just under four miles, beginning and ending at the entrance to the shrine. As the walk progressed, my thoughts of taking long walks with Amy slowly drifted away. By the two-mile mark, walking became more difficult, and by the time we turned into the driveway of the shrine, I wasn't sure I could make the last few steps to the van. Just as it happened with every training walk, by the end, I needed to crash into a chair finished for the day.

"Though my flesh and my heart fail, God is the rock of my heart, my portion forever." (Psalm 73:26)

-CHAPTER EIGHT-

Treasures

"He said, 'Then I beg you, father, send him to my father's house, for I have five brothers, so that he may warn them, lest they too come to this place of torment.'"
(Luke 16:27-28)

My thoughts turned to the healing service at Our Lady of Light Holy Spirit Center in Ohio and the woman who had frantically pulled down my socks and anointed my feet because she heard God tell her, "Ed is going to walk."

I did indeed walk 9.9 miles in around four hours, and not only that, we traveled over 1,600 miles in a van in less than three days. While it might not seem like much to most, either the walking or the driving would usually be impossible for me, and completing both in such a short time was unthinkable. Once again, God made the impossible possible. He showered His grace down upon me and healed me.

I saw it when I lived in the presence of the Holy Spirit, and I've seen it every day since. God's power is so great that

Triumph of the Cross

all things are indeed possible through Him if only we have faith, from passing a camel through the eye of a needle to commanding mountains to move. He has even allowed the lame like me to walk, carry my cross, and, for a brief time, carry His.

> *"Jesus looked at them and said, 'For human beings this is impossible, but for God all things are possible.'"*
> *(Matthew 19:26)*

I have given much thought to these most unlikely events of this pilgrimage. I've gone back to the morning of my fateful crash, where if anyone would have asked me then, "Are you going to heaven?" I would have given a resounding "Yes." At the time, I did not know I was but a fool, building up treasures here on earth without giving any thought or concern about storing up treasures for the Kingdom. God granted me tremendous mercy then, as He still does now, and He let me see the effects of sin on my soul.

Like the story of Lazarus the beggar and the rich man, I have been both men. Like the rich man, I lived in an eternity of misery and suffering, separated from the Lord, and like Lazarus, I have spent an eternity in the peace and joy of the glorious presence of God. But in His mercy for His children, the Lord allowed me to return and tell my brothers. This understanding brings me back to where I started and the question of storing treasure for the Kingdom.

Treasures

> *"Do not store up for yourselves treasures on earth, where moth and decay destroy, and thieves break in and steal. But store up treasures in heaven, where neither moth nor decay destroys, nor thieves break in and steal. For where your treasure is, there also will your heart be"*
> *(Matthew 6:19-21)*

I tell my story as often as I'm allowed, and I will speak to one solitary soul or to thousands at a time. I am compelled to help awaken those who are asleep, to introduce a spark into souls so that the Holy Spirit may breathe on them and grow that tiny spark into a blazing fire for the Lord.

I moved through much of my life without concern for building those treasures I desperately needed. I understand that any good I do now comes purely by the grace of God. Any spark I light, or soul I guide to the salvation of Christ comes not from me but rather from the Lord.

After walking on Operation True Cross, I asked the Lord to apply any treasures I may have stored through my apostolate toward the souls I've touched along the way. I lovingly offer my brothers and sisters my treasures in heaven. The Lord has gifted me with so much, and the Lord knows there was a time when I desperately needed treasures in the Kingdom, so now I give my treasures to those the Lord has touched through me. Christ did all the heavy lifting anyway, and He is the one who helps the people that I encounter. It seems unfair that I should take credit.

I trust in the divine justice of the Lord because I have already seen it with my own eyes. My judgment was just and deserving, and I agreed that I belonged in that place of eternal regret. I have also felt our Lord's divine love and mercy and wanted nothing more than to remain with Him forever. I pray that when I meet Him again, I hear Christ say, "Well done, Eddie."

"His master said to him, 'Well done, my good and faithful servant. Since you were faithful in small matters, I will give you great responsibilities. Come, share your master's joy.'"
(Matthew 25:23)

Bud and I departed the Shrine of Our Lady of Good Hope late that afternoon to bring me home. We discussed the incredible journey the Lord led us on and spoke of His and our zeal for souls. We prayed for all those we encountered on the way and gave praise and thanksgiving to God for the fantastic signs He had allowed us to witness. We decided that we made a good team for our Lord. With Bud and his great devotion to the Immaculate Heart of Mary and me with my great devotion to the Holy Spirit, her Spouse, it seemed that the Lord had drawn us together to do His work.

I hope the Lord will provide additional opportunities, as Bud says, "To claim as many souls for the Lord as we can." I look forward to whatever comes next for us, and I pray that the Lord will continue to bless both of our apostolates.

I pray that I may remain humble and remember that Christ is the one who does the work of saving souls. I pray that I continue to conform my will to the will of God. I pray that we will all share our stories of God with others and that we will spread the gospel to all we encounter by our example and actions.

Treasures

Wishing you blessings, calm winds, and blue skies.

"I have competed well; I have finished the race; I have kept the faith. From now on the crown of righteousness awaits me, which the Lord, the just judge, will award to me on that day, and not only to me, but to all who have longed for his appearance" (2 Timothy 4:7-8)

Acknowledgments

I must first thank God for the untold miracles He has lavished on me and continues to lavish upon me. I am grateful for the many of His friends He has sent to join me on the way.

Thanks to...

- My family and friends who have cared for and supported me during my never-ending recovery.
- The church groups, friends, and neighbors who have welcomed my story into their hearts and helped me spread God's message.
- The medical personnel, who, through God's grace, have helped me to cope with chronic pain.
- All the faithful around the world who continue to pray for me, my family, and my apostolate.
- I'd like to thank my friend and priest, Father Dale Ehrman, for helping me understand the messages God has given me and ensuring I tell the story correctly.

Triumph of the Cross

- Thanks to Bud Macfarlane and the Mary Foundation for inviting me to talk and walk with them.
- Thanks to Laura Zeck for her help in creating the cover and for formatting this book.
- Thank you to the long list of people who have helped me along the way. It seems the Lord places another person along my path each day to help guide me to Him.

I pray daily for anyone who has read, listened to, or watched my story. May God bless you.

themysticnextdoor1@gmail.com

or

edjozsa@presenceofGodencounters.com

PresenceOfGodEncounters.com

About Ed Jozsa

Ed Jozsa was born and raised Catholic in Western Pennsylvania, just north of Pittsburgh. While attending his parish youth group he fell in love with a beautiful girl named Amy. Ed and Amy were married and became the proud parents of three children. They are now members of Our Lady of Grace Catholic Church, Noblesville, IN.

Ed started his flying career as a flight instructor and obtained his bachelor's degree in aeronautics from Embry Riddle University. Ed was a captain for three airlines through the years and ended his career as a Boeing 767 captain for FedEx. Ed was an airline pilot for 28 years, totaling over 13,000 hours in the air. He is now medically retired

Triumph of the Cross

Ed was the last person to expect a mystical vision, but a near-death experience after a catastrophic auto accident brought him closer to God than he ever imagined. Ed wrote a book, The Mystic Next Door, an Ordinary Man's Extraordinary Encounter with the Holy Spirit, where he tells of his experience of miracles, terrifying as well as heavenly visions, and how it transformed his view of life, faith, eternity, and the Holy Trinity.

Ed now gives talks around the country and shares his experience with God. He operates a website where people can read a daily devotional, find his book, or share their own stories of personal encounters with God. Read Ed's story or watch his story on his website, www.presenceofGodencounters.com, and ask yourself, how is God working through me, calling out to me, and awakening me to His will?

Want to Dive Deeper?

Visit Ed's website: www.presenceofGodencounters.com
From there you'll be able to:

- Get your copy of his first book, *The Mystic Next Door: An Ordinary Man's Extraordinary Encounter with the Holy Spirit*.

- Sign up for his newsletter, Fingerprints of the Holy Spirit, to receive daily inspiration as well as the latest updates and announcements.

- Donate to Ed's apostolate, Presence of God Encounters.

- Check out all the upcoming events where Ed will be speaking.

- Request Ed to come speak at your event.